COLPs To

Related titles from Law Society Publishing:

Anti-Bribery Toolkit
Amy Bell

COFAs Toolkit
Jeremy Black and Florence Perret du Cray

Outcomes-Focused Regulation
Andrew Hopper QC and Gregory Treverton-Jones QC

The Solicitor's Handbook 2012
Andrew Hopper QC and Gregory Treverton-Jones QC

All books from Law Society Publishing can be ordered through good bookshops or direct from our distributors, Prolog, by telephone 0870 850 1422 or e-mail **lawsociety@prolog.uk.com**. Please confirm the price before ordering.

For further information or a catalogue, please contact our editorial and marketing office by e-mail **publishing@lawsociety.org.uk**.

COLPs Toolkit

Michelle Garlick

The Law Society

Material in Annex 4F is reproduced from Practical Law Company with the permission of the publishers. For further information, visit www.practicallaw.com.

ISBN 978-1-907698-46-0

Published in 2012 by the Law Society
113 Chancery Lane, London WC2A 1PL

Reprinted in 2012 (twice) and 2013 (twice)

Typeset by Columns Design XML Ltd, Reading
Printed by TJ International Ltd, Padstow, Cornwall

The paper used for the text pages of this book is FSC® certified. FSC (the Forest Stewardship Council®) is an international network to promote responsible management of the world's forests.

FSC
www.fsc.org
MIX
Paper from
responsible sources
FSC® C013056

Contents

Foreword

While it is fair to say that many firms have been identifying and managing risks for a long time, the demands of the Legal Services Act 2007 and the Solicitors Regulation Authority's introduction of outcomes-focused regulation mean that all firms – whatever their shape, size or location – must prioritise risk management.

Instead of adhering to a precise set of rules the profession is now working toward a list of outcomes, supported by indicative behaviours, and this change in approach brings with it a greater focus on regulating the practice as well as the individual solicitor.

To help firms meet their legal and regulatory obligations, the Law Society established its Risk and Compliance Service a little over a year and a half ago. To date, the Service's compliance support includes bespoke in-house consultancy, webinars, monthly e-newsletters, master classes, seminars and conferences.

It is important for solicitors to be aware that they will not need to re-work all their systems and procedures in the light of the SRA Code of Conduct 2011. This is particularly pertinent for sole practitioners, who are often the senior partner, law firm manager and risk professional rolled into one.

With these things in mind, the Law Society's Risk and Compliance Service in collaboration with a number of subject matter experts has commissioned this series of hands-on toolkits.

These practical guides have been prepared with the busy practitioner in mind. They aim to help reduce the cost of compliance for practitioners by providing a useful set of reference notes, definitions, best practice tips and templates. Much of their content is informed by first-hand information gleaned through onsite risk diagnostic visits and interactions with members of the profession, and in response to practitioner requests for tools to assist in their compliance journey.

Our hope is that these toolkits rapidly become 'must-have' elements in every practitioner's compliance armoury and to this end I recommend them to you without reservation.

The Risk and Compliance Service would like to thank the author, Michelle Garlick at Weightmans LLP, for her contribution to the *COLPs Toolkit*.

Pearl Moses
Risk and Compliance Manager
The Law Society

Preface

On 6 October 2011, the new SRA Handbook came into force. It marked a significant change in the approach of the Solicitors Regulation Authority (SRA) to regulation, moving from one which was rules-based to one which is outcomes-focused. There is now much greater emphasis on compliance with principles and outcomes, and also effective management. This is where the new roles of the compliance officer for legal practice (COLP) and the compliance officer for finance and administration (COFA) come into play.

It is the introduction of these two new roles into firms which has prompted us to write this book. The focus of this toolkit is on the role of the COLP (a separate toolkit has been published for the COFA) but there will undoubtedly need to be frequent communication between the COLP and COFA regarding risks, breaches arising and the need to report issues to the SRA.

The aim of this toolkit is to provide practical guidance and templates to give the COLP a 'head start' in taking on this new role. Areas covered include the process for becoming a COLP, how to ensure compliance within the firm and dealing with your reporting obligations.

Of course, every firm is different and already at different levels of compliance. One size does not fit all, but it is hoped that the toolkit will help you and your firm move towards compliance with the specific requirements expected of the COLP as set out in the SRA Handbook.

This toolkit is based on the law and SRA regulatory requirements as at 23 April 2012. At the time of going to press, the SRA have stated that a web-based nomination form for COLPs and COFAs will be available from **www.sra.org.uk** from 31 May 2012 with nominations to be submitted by 31 July 2012.

I would like to take this opportunity to thank my colleagues Nicola Whitehouse and James Holman for their valued contributions to this toolkit.

Good luck in your new role!

Michelle Garlick
Partner, Weightmans LLP
April 2012

1 Role of the COLP

On 6 October 2011, the new SRA Handbook came into force. It marked a significant change in the approach of the Solicitors Regulation Authority (SRA) to regulation, from being rules-based to being outcomes-focused. The emphasis is now on more general, high-level principles and outcomes, which when achieved will benefit clients, as well as on effective management. The new regulations also include an obligation on an authorised body to have a compliance officer for legal' practice (COLP) and a compliance officer for finance and administration (COFA).

The SRA has created the role of the COLP to act as a direct contact between the authorised body and the SRA with regard to compliance. Each authorised body must be able to demonstrate how it is achieving compliance. This means that the COLP must have policies, procedures and records in place to document each step taken in connection with the firm's compliance and risk management requirements. In essence, each authorised body will need an audit trail to justify its actions.

The responsibilities of the COLP will be significant and many will view them as onerous. The COLP (with help from the other partners/members of the firm) must ensure compliance is part of the firm's culture. It is not just about policies and procedures; the minds of managers, fee earners and support staff will all have to be trained to think 'compliance' at every step. Staff should also feel that they are able to report breaches to the COLP, be they big or small, and feel comfortable doing so.

1.1 The COLP's responsibilities

The responsibilities being placed on the COLP are broad. Furthermore, the COLP could potentially face personal liability for failing to implement a compliance regime. It is therefore important that the right person is chosen to be the firm's COLP. We consider who can be the COLP in **Chapter 2**.

The role and the requirements of the COLP are contained in rule 8.5 of the SRA Authorisation Rules for Legal Services Bodies and Licensable Bodies 2011 ('the SRA Authorisation Rules'), although, of course, the COLP will also need to have regard to the SRA Handbook as a whole (see below). Rule 8.5 is set out in **Appendix A**. To summarise, the COLP has three key responsibilities:

1. **to ensure compliance with the terms and conditions of their firm's authorisation.** The SRA's regulatory arrangements include all rules and regulations set by the SRA in relation to: authorisation; practice; conduct; discipline; qualification of persons carrying on legal activities; and the indemnification and compensation arrangements. COLPs must therefore be familiar with the general conditions placed upon the firm and its employees as well as any additional conditions

placed on their firm's authorisation/licence. Ensuring compliance with the SRA Accounts Rules 2011 will be the responsibility of the COFA;

2.   **to ensure compliance with statutory obligations,** e.g. duties imposed by the Legal Services Act 2007, the Solicitors Act 1974 and the Administration of Justice Act 1985; and

3.   **to report to the SRA any failure so to comply.** This is a twofold obligation: the first duty is to report any material failures as soon as reasonably practicable; the second is to report non-material failures as part of the annual information report required under rule 8.7 of the SRA Authorisation Rules.

Ensuring compliance is considered in **Chapter 3** and we consider the issues of reporting and recording breaches in **Chapter 4.**

Rule 8 of the SRA Authorisation Rules details the general conditions of authorisation including:

- ensuring compliance with the regulatory arrangements;
- ensuring that suitable arrangements are in place to ensure compliance;
- paying a periodical fee;
- having a COLP and a COFA; and
- providing the SRA with an annual information report.

The COLP must also be aware of other specific parts of the SRA Handbook including, but not limited to:

- Principles 7 and 8;
- Chapter 7 of the SRA Code of Conduct 2011 – Management of your business; and
- Chapter 10 of the SRA Code of Conduct 2011 – You and your regulator.

Regulatory action can be taken against COLPs for failing to meet their responsibilities, although the SRA has said that it will not make the COLP the scapegoat and that ultimately the firm is responsible. It is for this reason that the COLP must be chosen carefully and must be in a position to carry out their role effectively. Whilst compliance still ultimately lies with the managers of the practice, situations could arise in which the COLP has to report issues to the SRA against the managers' wishes. A COLP must be given the authority to do this.

Suggested wording providing such authority can be found in **Annex 2B.** This is not essential as the COLP's statutory authority is set out in the SRA Authorisation Rules. We have included it as some COLPs may wish to have the comfort of a signed authority from the firm.

1.2 Overseas practice

Specific references to overseas practice are made throughout the SRA Handbook. The Law Society has issued a practice note listing all the provisions related to overseas practice in one place. It also sets out any changes in the overseas provisions from the Solicitors' Code of Conduct 2007: **www.lawsociety.org.uk/ productsandservices/practicenotes/overseaspractice.page**.

2 Becoming a COLP

2.1 Who can be a COLP?

To be a COLP the individual must:

- be a lawyer of England and Wales; registered European lawyer (REL) or European lawyer regulated by the Bar Standards Board (BSB);
- be an employee or a manager of the firm;
- be of sufficient seniority and in a position of sufficient responsibility to fulfil the role;
- be approved by the SRA as the COLP;
- consent to undertake the role;
- not have been disqualified from acting as a head of legal practice (HOLP) as defined by the Legal Services Act 2007; and
- be authorised to do one or more of the reserved activities specified in the firm's certificate of authorisation.

The SRA Handbook Glossary 2012 provides the following definitions:

lawyer of England and Wales means:

(i)   a solicitor, or
(ii) an individual who is authorised to carry on legal activities in England and Wales by an approved regulator other than the SRA, but excludes a member of an Establishment Directive profession registered with the BSB under the Establishment Directive [98/5/EC].

...

manager means:

(i)   a member of an LLP;
(ii) a director of a company;
(iii) a partner in a partnership; or
(iv) in relation to any other body, a member of its governing body.

The SRA has not provided a definition or guidance as to the meaning of 'sufficiently senior' or 'in a position of sufficient responsibility'. However, guidance note (vi) to rule 8 of the SRA Authorisation Rules states that the COLP's role is:

a fundamental part of a firm's compliance and governance arrangements ... The firm must therefore ensure that any person designated as its COLP ... is of sufficient seniority, in a position of sufficient power and responsibility and has clear reporting lines to enable them to have access to all management systems and arrangements and all other relevant information including client files and business information.

Who should be chosen as the COLP will depend upon the size and nature of the firm. The SRA has hinted that larger firms should think carefully before appointing their managing partner as their COLP. For smaller firms and sole practitioners, the managing partner may be the only or obvious choice. (See 'A brave new world: expectations for outcomes-focused regulation', opening speech to the 'Risk and management for law firms' conference by Samantha Barrass, 6 December 2011; **www.sra.org.uk/documents/SRA/news/9-december-speech.pdf**.)

Whilst the same person can be both the COLP and the COFA, that person must have the necessary skills and knowledge (and, of course, time) to fulfil both roles.

If any aspect of compliance (but not responsibility) is to be delegated to others within the firm, the COLP will need to ensure that this is monitored and there is a clear line of reporting between the person carrying out the function and the COLP.

> Firms should also think carefully about the personality traits needed to be able to fulfil the role of the COLP. A draft job description is included at **Annex 2A**.

2.2 SRA approval of the COLP

Part 4 of the SRA Authorisation Rules deals with the approval process for the COLP.

The SRA may approve a COLP if it is satisfied, in accordance with Part 4 of the SRA Authorisation Rules, that the individual is a suitable person to carry out his or her duties (rule 8.5(f) of the SRA Authorisation Rules). Part 4 of the SRA Authorisation Rules is provided at **Appendix A**.

The COLP must meet the criteria set out in the SRA Suitability Test 2011 (see **Appendix B**) in order to be approved and the prospective COLP is under an obligation to submit evidence of their suitability to the SRA. Specifically, the prospective COLP should disclose information as to:

- offences involving dishonesty;
- offences involving violence;
- disciplinary findings; and
- disqualification as a company director or trustee of a charity.

The SRA can and may look at the honesty and integrity of those connected with and related to the COLP where it has reason to believe that that person has an influence over the way the candidate will exercise their role.

For approval, the SRA also requires the COLP to:

- co-operate in providing documentation and giving information; and
- provide a declaration that the information is correct and complete.

Firms will be able to nominate COLPs (and COFAs) from 31 May 2012 until 31 July 2012 and approval will be given by the SRA by 31 December 2012. Compliance officers will start fulfilling their duties on 1 January 2013.

To nominate its COLP, the firm will complete a web-based nomination form that sets out the obligations of the firm under rules 8.1, 8.2 and 8.5 of the SRA Authorisation Rules and the responsibilities of the COLP under rule 8.5(c). It is based on binding declarations by both a manager with authority to sign on behalf of the firm and the COLP nominee.

The firm's side of the declaration, signed by a manager, includes confirmation that:

- the firm has suitable arrangements in place to ensure that the COLP is able to discharge their duties; and
- the COLP's declarations, including that the nominee has sufficient seniority and responsibility in the firm, are correct.

The COLP nominee declares that:

- they understand their obligations and have sufficient responsibility in the firm and are in a position of sufficient seniority to perform the role;
- they are satisfied that the firm's managers have put in place suitable arrangements to ensure that they are able to discharge the COLP duties in accordance with the rules;
- they will take all reasonable steps to ensure compliance; and
- they consent to being designated as the COLP.

The nomination form also includes questions drawn from the SRA Suitability Test (see **Appendix B**).

Note: This section on the nomination process is based on the information published on the SRA website at the time of going to press. The SRA has indicated that it will contact all firms and provide further advice and information including obligations placed on those completing the forms. For up-to-date guidance on the nomination process and the information to be provided to the SRA, refer to the SRA website: **www.sra.org.uk.**

The SRA has also made provision for the temporary emergency approval of a COLP in circumstances where the firm's COLP is unable to fulfil the role, for example, due to long term illness.

A precedent notification letter to the SRA applying for temporary emergency approval can be found at **Annex 2D**.

2.3 The COLP and the firm

The role of the COLP is new and unchartered. It will not have been considered when the two parties negotiated their employment contract and/or partnership agreement. On this basis, formal provisions may need to be considered, especially bearing in mind that the COLP will be expected to report issues to the SRA even when it is against the wishes of the firm's management. The authority of the COLP to do this is set out in the SRA Authorisation Rules and some COLPs may feel that this gives them sufficient authority; others may wish to obtain the firm's management's written authority.

> Some suggested wording for terms of appointment is provided in **Annex 2B.**

Depending on the size and nature of the firm, some firms may also consider obtaining a signed confirmation from each partner that they understand their personal obligations to comply with the SRA Handbook, that they give the COLP their authority to report breaches to the SRA and that they will not obstruct the COLP in doing so.

> A suggested confirmation agreement from the individual partners can be found at **Annex 2C.**

The guidance notes to rule 8 of the SRA Authorisation Rules make it clear that the existence and the requirements of the COLP are not a substitute for the firm's and managers' responsibilities and obligations. Ultimate responsibility rests with the managers and owners. However, personal liability could attach to, and regulatory action be taken against, the COLP where they fail to meet their responsibilities. Firms and COLPs alike may therefore wish to consider including indemnity provisions for such circumstances. Such indemnities will inevitably be limited in scope, for example, perhaps covering financial sanctions only and will not protect against such sanctions as reprimands or, at the other end of the scale, the removal of a person's practising certificate or the removal of the person as the COLP.

COLPs may feel that without some protection, they will not wish to 'consent'. Director and Officer or Management Liability cover may be available and COLPs and the firm should discuss availability of such cover with brokers. Care should be taken to check any exclusions in the policy. Firms too will want to protect themselves and ensure that they do not have to provide an indemnity when a COLP has knowingly been reckless or fraudulent or acted with wilful neglect.

The granting of indemnities is not straightforward and firms may wish to take further advice regarding this.

Finally, firms should ensure that their compliance policy runs alongside their internal disciplinary proceedings policy to ensure that all employees and managers are aware of the obligation to comply with the SRA's new regulations, follow the procedures and policies of the firm and report any breaches to the COLP (see **Chapter 4**).

Annex 2A
Draft job description

> **Note:** This is an example only and it will depend upon the size and nature of your firm as to the type of characteristics you will need the COLP to have.

Job title

Compliance officer for legal practice (COLP)

Role

- Act as a channel of communication between the firm and the Solicitors Regulation Authority (SRA) regarding compliance.
- Develop, initiate, maintain, and revise policies and procedures for risk management and compliance.
- Manage the day-to-day operation of the compliance programme.
- Direct compliance issues to the appropriate resources for investigation and resolution. This may involve collaborating with other departments and people, such as: risk management, internal audit, human resources (HR), IT, finance, the compliance officer for finance and administration (COFA), the money laundering reporting officer (MLRO), the data protection officer (DPO), etc.
- Monitor, record and report, as necessary, any breaches of compliance.
- Respond to alleged breaches of rules, regulations and policies.
- Remain up to date regarding the firm's compliance obligations.
- Identify potential areas of compliance vulnerability and risk; develop and implement corrective action plans for resolution of problematic issues, and provide general guidance on how to avoid or deal with similar situations in the future.
- Monitor the performance of the compliance regime and review policies on a continuing basis, taking appropriate steps to improve their effectiveness.
- Act as an internal resource with whom concerned employees may communicate and seek advice.
- Report, on a regular basis, and as directed or requested, to [the board/senior management] with regard to the operation and progress of compliance efforts.
- Work with HR and others, as appropriate, to develop an effective compliance training programme, including appropriate introductory training for new employees as well as ongoing training for all employees and managers.

Qualifications

Any person applying to be the COLP must:

- be a lawyer of England or Wales; registered European lawyer (REL) or European lawyer regulated by the Bar Standards Board;
- be a partner or employee in a senior position of responsibility;
- meet the criteria set out in the SRA Suitability Test 2011;
- be authorised to do one or more of the reserved activities specified in the firm's certificate of authorisation.

Required skills and knowledge

Any person applying to be the COLP must:

- have excellent knowledge of the SRA Handbook;
- have excellent knowledge of compliance requirements;
- be commercially aware, astute and proactive in developing ideas and solutions;
- have well-developed project management, time management and organisational skills;
- have well-developed persuading and influencing skills;
- be confident, assertive and resilient;
- have excellent interpersonal and communication skills (written and oral).

Annex 2B
Authority from the firm/terms of appointment

TERMS OF APPOINTMENT AND CONSENT TO THE POSITION OF COMPLIANCE OFFICER FOR LEGAL PRACTICE ('COLP') OF [*NAME OF FIRM*] ('THE FIRM')

The Firm's obligations

The Firm:

1. will provide adequate facilities and resources to allow the COLP to fulfil their obligations under the SRA Authorisation Rules for Legal Services Bodies and Licensable Bodies 2011 (the SRA Authorisation Rules) and under this Appointment;
2. will ensure that the COLP has access to all necessary information and will be granted the necessary authority to exercise effectively the responsibilities of the COLP;
3. will ensure that no manager or employee of the Firm obstructs the COLP in their role as COLP and that the COLP will have direct access to the Firm's [board/management committee/senior partner];
4. hereby authorises the COLP to report to the SRA as soon as reasonably practicable any material breach of the SRA Handbook, SRA Code of Conduct or other regulatory or statutory obligation which the SRA Authorisation Rules require should be reported by a COLP to the SRA and waives any right of action against the COLP for damages or loss resulting from any such reports which are made in good faith even though it may subsequently transpire that the COLP was mistaken in the belief that there was cause for concern[; and]
[5. agrees to provide the COLP with an indemnity for any [financial sanction,] [defence costs (including the costs of separate legal advice where necessary),] [or disbursements] arising from any investigation, inquiry or proceedings brought by the SRA against the COLP personally PROVIDED ALWAYS that the COLP has at all times acted in their role as COLP with good faith and with reasonable due care and attention].

The COLP's obligations

As COLP I agree to:

1. take all reasonable steps to ensure compliance with the terms of the Firm's authorisation by the Firm, its employees and managers;
2. take all reasonable steps to ensure the Firm's compliance with the relevant regulatory arrangements;
3. take all reasonable steps to ensure the Firm's compliance with relevant statutory obligations;
4. record details of and, as soon as reasonably practicable, report to the SRA any failure to comply where such failure is material on its own or as part of a pattern; and

5. record details of any non-material failure to comply and include this information in the annual report to the SRA.

Signed on behalf of the Firm

_____

Signature

_____

Name and position, printed

_____

Date

COLP's consent

I hereby accept appointment as the COLP of the Firm on the terms set out above and confirm that I have the necessary skills and experience to take on this role.

_____

Signature

_____

Name and position, printed

_____

Date

Annex 2C
Individual partner's authority

I, [*name of partner*], hereby confirm that I will comply (and use best endeavours to ensure compliance by all personnel supervised by me) with all statutes, regulations, professional standards and other provisions as may from time to time govern the conduct of the firm or be determined by [*name of firm*] as standards to be voluntarily applied by [*name of firm*] including the firm's risk management and quality procedures. I also confirm that I will not in any way obstruct the compliance officer for legal practice (COLP) and compliance officer for finance and administration (COFA) in fulfilling their roles and hereby authorise the COLP and COFA to report any material breaches to the Solicitors Regulation Authority in accordance with the requirements of the SRA Authorisation Rules for Legal Services Bodies and Licensable Bodies 2011.

_____

Signature

_____

Name, printed

_____

Date

Annex 2D

Notification and temporary emergency approval application letter to the SRA

[Firm's contact details]

Solicitors Regulation Authority
Ipsley Court
Berrington Close
Redditch
Worcestershire
B98 0TD

[Date]

Your ref: *[SRA ref]*
Our ref: *[internal ref]*

Dear Sirs

We write to advise you that our existing COLP, *[name]*, is currently unable to fulfil [his/her] role due to *[set out circumstances]*. In accordance with rule 18 of the SRA Authorisation Rules for Legal Services Bodies and Licensable Bodies 2011, we are writing to notify you of our designation of *[name of temporary replacement]* as the COLP and hereby apply for temporary emergency approval of *[name of temporary replacement]*.

Please acknowledge receipt of this notification with confirmation that temporary approval has been granted.

We look forward to hearing from you.

Yours faithfully

3 Ensuring compliance

In this section, we consider the COLP's responsibilities for ensuring compliance.

To ensure that compliance is enshrined within the firm, policies and procedures will need to be implemented, reviewed and monitored for compliance and then improved upon where necessary. The SRA has provided guidance on the systems that it will expect to see in place in every practice.

The key to meeting the requirements of the role is to keep a record – an audit trail – of monitoring. This record keeping will be crucial in illustrating to the SRA that the COLP has been fulfilling the role. It is important to remember that the COLP will not be personally liable for breaches per se, but could be liable for failing to implement, or for failing to illustrate that they have implemented, systems to avoid such breaches.

3.1 Compliance plan

In guidance note (iii) to rule 8 of the SRA Authorisation Rules, the SRA highlights that firms should have suitable arrangements for compliance with the SRA's regulatory requirements (a 'compliance plan'). (See also Chapter 7 of the SRA Code of Conduct.) What needs to be covered by the compliance plan will depend on factors such as the size and nature of the practice, its work and its areas of risk. According to the guidance note, common areas which the SRA expects to see in a compliance plan include:

(a) clearly defined governance arrangements providing a transparent framework for responsibilities within the firm;
(b) appropriate accounting procedures;
(c) a system for ensuring that only the appropriate people authorise payments from client account;
(d) a system for ensuring that undertakings are given only when intended, and that compliance with them is monitored and enforced;
(e) appropriate checks on new staff or contractors;
(f) a system for ensuring that basic regulatory deadlines are not missed, e.g. submission of the firm's accountant's report, arranging indemnity cover, renewal of practising certificates and registrations, renewal of all lawyers' licences to practise and provision of regulatory information;
(g) a system for monitoring, reviewing and managing risks;
(h) ensuring that issues of conduct are given appropriate weight in decisions the firm takes, whether on client matters or firm-based issues such as funding;
(i) file reviews;
(j) appropriate systems for supporting the development and training of staff;
(k) obtaining the necessary approvals of managers, owners and COLP/COFA [see **www.sra.org.uk/solicitors/pc-registration-renewal/notifications/nml.page** for guidance on obtaining advance approval of new managers and owners];

(l)   arrangements to ensure that any duties to clients and others are fully met even when staff are absent.

The compliance plan should be used to identify and understand the firm's practice areas, clients, business strategy, etc. From this, the COLP will be able to assess the areas of risk and identify policies and procedures which can target and reduce the risk of non-compliance.

Whilst a compliance plan is not mandatory (it is referred to in non-mandatory guidance notes), firms which choose not to use one must ask themselves whether and how they will be able to show that they have suitable arrangements in place to ensure compliance.

A compliance plan can take many formats and is unique to each and every firm, so providing a general precedent within this toolkit is not possible. However, at **Annex 3A** there is a draft outline of a compliance plan which includes suggested areas, topics and questions each firm should consider. An office manual setting out the firm's procedures and policies would equally suffice provided it covers all the regulatory requirements.

In any event, the office manual or compliance plan should be a live, working document which the COLP takes overall control of reviewing. The COLP must also ensure that what is said within the office manual or compliance plan is actually done in practice.

3.2 Risk register

Whilst there is no obligation to have a risk register, Chapter 7 of the SRA Code of Conduct (at O(7.3)) requires that 'you identify, monitor and manage risks to compliance with all the Principles, rules and outcomes and other requirements of the Handbook, if applicable to you, and take steps to address issues identified ...'. Having a risk register will enable the COLP to do this.

COLPs should use the risk register as a tool to identify, assess and manage risks down to acceptable levels. The register provides a framework in which problems that threaten client services and the business are highlighted. Actions can then be instigated to reduce the probability and potential impact of specific risks.

The COLP should seek input from personnel from various departments (including department heads, managers and support workers). Different departments will face different risks which will have a variety of impacts on the department involved and on the wider firm.

An example risk register is shown at Table 3.1. The template is provided at **Annex 3B**.

Table 3.1 Example risk register

Note: The examples in this risk register will not cover all of the risks that your firm faces. The risk register must be individually tailored to your firm and risks considered in context.

Risk identified	Potential consequences	Impact (high/ medium/ low)	Probability (high/ medium/ low)	Overall risk (high/ medium/ low)	Response	Action plan	Owner	Delivery date	Review date	Notes
Client care										
Client engagement letters:										
• Content	Complaints /claims/ costs recovery	High	Medium	High	Partners only sign client care letters having checked properly scoped and costed	Review client engagement letters to ensure compliance with outcomes				
• Not sent out		High	Medium	High	Reminder system in case management software					
Client dissatisfaction	Complaints to LeO/SRA	High	Low	Medium	File reviews	Monthly review of complaints arising				
Complaints handling	LeO case fees	High	Low	Medium	Complaints policy	Review complaints policy	COLP/ complaints partner			
Inadequate resources	Delay in service to client	High	Medium	Medium/ high		Review resources				
Inaccurate costs estimates	Complaints/ write-offs	High	Medium	Medium/ high	Costs updates to clients	Training to staff on costs advice/ estimates				

Risk	Consequence				Control	Action	Owner	Frequency
Case management								
Misunderstanding client objectives	Claims/ complaints	Medium	Medium	Medium	Scoping of retainer and regular advice to clients	Provide training		
Failing to meet key deadlines	Claims	Medium	High	Medium/ high	Key date procedures diary and back-up diary			
Non-compliance with undertakings procedures	Breach of undertakings – disciplinary and claims consequences	High	Low	Medium	Undertaking policy	Set up central register for undertakings	COLP	Monthly
Conduct/regulatory/compliance								
Non-compliance with practising certificate requirements	Unable to practise	High	Low	Low	Record keeping	Diarise key dates/liaise with HR	COLP	
Non-compliance with professional Indemnity Insurance (PII)		High	Low	Low/ medium	Broker assistance	Diarise and liaise with brokers		
Conflict/confidentiality								
Failure to or inadequate check for conflicts	Wasted costs/ loss of client	Medium	Medium	Medium	Conflicts policy and systems	Review conflicts policy; Provide training on conflicts procedures	COLP	
Conflicts arising	Cease acting	High	Low	Medium		Set up COLP authority record of decisions to act/no conflict	COLP	

Risk identified	Potential consequences	Impact (high/ medium/ low)	Probability (high/ medium/ low)	Overall risk (high/ medium/ low)	Response	Action plan	Owner	Delivery date	Review date	Notes
Money laundering/fraud										
Non-compliance with money laundering regulations	Exposure to litigation/ prosecution	High	Low	Medium	Anti-money laundering procedures	Staff training	MLRO			
Data protection										
Non-compliance with data protection regulations	Breach of client confidentiality/ claims	Medium	Medium	Medium	Data protection procedures	Staff training	DPO			
Loss of files, documents, deeds, wills, etc.		Low	Low	Low	Policy on removal of files	Staff training/ safe storage				
Removal of files from the office		High	Medium	High	Policy on removal of files	Staff training/ awareness				
Destruction of files, documents		Low	Low	Low	Policy on destruction of files, documents	Staff training/ awareness				
Protection of personal ID, bank details		Medium	Low	Low/ medium	Policy on personal ID, bank details					
Training and competence										
Non-compliance with CPD rules	Failure to maintain expertise	Low	Low	Low	Training and record keeping	Set up central record keeping	HR			
Health and safety										
Non-compliance with health and safety regulations	Injury to staff/ visitors; Exposure to litigation/ prosecution	Low	Medium	Medium	Health and safety procedures	Health and safety audits	HR			

Risk	Consequence				Control	Action
Discrimination, diversity and equality						
Non-compliance with anti-discrimination legislation and SRA Code of Conduct, Ch.2	Exposure to litigation	Low	Low	Low	Anti-discrimination policy Equality and diversity policy Recruitment procedures	
Financial control						
Non-compliance with Financial Services Authority (FSA) rules (see Specialist service rules)	Disciplinary	Low	Low	Low	Registration	Check registered on the FSA exempt professional firms (EPF) register
Non-compliance with SRA Accounts Rules		High	Medium	Medium/ high	Finance procedures	Staff training Regular review meetings with COFA
Business continuity						
Loss of key personnel	Loss of income Business interruption	High	Low	Medium		Locum policy/ emergency approval of COLP/ COFA
Catastrophic event	Physical damage to premises and client papers	High	Low	Medium	Business continuity plan	
Financial stability						
Market forces	Closure of business/ expensive run-off cover	High	Medium	Medium/ high		Consider merger partner/ successor practice?

3.3 Gap analysis

A gap analysis means reviewing the firm's current policies and procedures against the principles and outcomes set out in the SRA Handbook. It is useful for identifying areas of weakness within the firm. A gap analysis allows the COLP to set out where the firm is, where it needs and wants to be and how it is going to get there, whilst ensuring it remains client focused. Be careful however of what the SRA has called 'unthinking compliance', i.e. a tick-box exercise, going through all the indicative behaviours of the SRA Code of Conduct (which are non-mandatory) without thinking of the clients' needs.

A gap analysis spreadsheet is provided at **Annex 3C.**

3.4 Monthly monitoring by the COLP

COLPs should also carry out a monthly review of the risk register and document their findings.

A suggested monthly compliance monitoring form is provided at **Annex 3D.**

Close liaison with the complaints partner (if a different person) and the COFA will be necessary in order to identify trends or patterns which require reporting, and will also help to identify areas needing improvement and staff training requirements.

A template for recording reviews with the complaints partner is provided at **Annex 3E.**

Annex 3A
Draft compliance plan

> **Note:** This narrative form is just one example of how a compliance plan can be presented. It should be used to direct the firm's staff to relevant existing procedures and systems, either via links (if the plan is on the intranet) or by reference to page numbers within an office or risk manual. It will also need to tie in with the firm's risk register.

[*Name of firm*]'s statement of compliance

In October 2011, the Solicitors Regulation Authority (SRA) introduced the SRA Handbook. To ensure compliance with the principles, outcomes and other requirements of the new SRA Handbook, as well as with our statutory obligations, appropriate systems and controls are in place. This compliance plan sets out the firm's commitment to ensuring compliance and provides staff members with an overview of the policies and procedures that are in place to identify, monitor and manage risks.

Risk profile

History and ownership of the firm

[*Brief overview of when the firm was set up and the structure of the firm. It may be helpful to include an organisational chart illustrating firm reporting lines.*]

Strategic objectives of the firm

[*Brief overview of the firm's strategy and targets, as these will have a bearing on the risks it will face. For example, the quicker a firm intends to grow the more susceptible it will be to risk.*]

Size of firm

[*Number of partners, employees, etc.*]

Type of work, firm's markets and client base

[*Summary of the departments and the clients of the firm, e.g. sophisticated and/or unsophisticated users of legal services.*]

Level of risk for work

[Low/Medium/High]

The firm's locations

[*e.g. foreign jurisdictions, multiple locations within England and Wales, High Street, legal aid practice, etc.*]

Quality/make-up of staff

[*e.g. level/types of qualifications, etc. – some levels/types may require increased supervision.*]

Work within regulated and/or unregulated sectors

[*i.e. for the purposes of the Money Laundering Regulations 2007.*]

Managing the business

Governance structure

[*What structure is in place to manage the firm? What does the firm have in place in the way of boards, committees or individual roles? What reporting lines are in place? Confirmation that issues of conduct are given appropriate weight in decisions the firm takes, whether on client matters or firm-based issues such as funding.*]

Business plan

[*Overview of the firm's business plan and its connection with risk and compliance.*]

Managing compliance

[*Refer to and identify the COLP. How is risk managed within the firm? What procedures and policies are in place? Where can policies and procedures be located? How is compliance monitored? Who is trained in compliance? Who can employees ask to seek training? Who is responsible for the management of risk? Who is responsible for ensuring regulatory deadlines are not missed? Who is responsible for obtaining approvals of managers/owners, COLP and COFA?*]

Financial management

[*Refer to and identify the COFA. Who is responsible for managing the financial risks? What procedures and policies are in place for managing financial risk? What accounting procedures are in place? Who can authorise payments from client account?*]

Training

[*Who is responsible for training employees? This may be several people, covering e.g. complaints, money laundering, data protection, SRA Accounts Rules, CPD. What induction training do you give? What training and development plans are in place?*]

Supervision

[*What supervision procedures are in place? Include reference to day-to-day supervision, file review and audit procedures.*]

HR

[*What procedures are in place to carry out appropriate checks on new staff and contractors? What health and safety procedures does the firm have? What arrangements are in place to ensure that duties to clients and others are fully met even when staff are absent?*]

Undertakings

[*What policy is in place to ensure that undertakings are only given when intended and that compliance with them is monitored and enforced?*]

Compliance obligations

[*Name of firm*] is committed to ensuring compliance with regulatory requirements and managing risk. Failure to comply with regulatory requirements can have serious consequences such as:

- clients not receiving the level of service to which they are entitled (for example, where the firm fails to meet their expectations), which may result in client complaints and negligence claims;
- damage to our reputation;
- the firm and/or individuals opening themselves up to being disciplined by the SRA or another regulator, which could result in fines and/or disqualification;
- the firm and/or individuals exposing themselves to criminal prosecution.

The firm has an open door policy and encourages its employees to share their thoughts and feelings regarding compliance. Employees are under an obligation to report any breaches of compliance to the COLP.

All employees have responsibility for managing their own risk and compliance. All employees must ensure they are familiar with this compliance plan.

The firm's compliance plan is constantly under review. The COLP is responsible for changes to it and any changes will be communicated to all staff.

The firm's compliance obligations are broad and include but are not limited to the:

- SRA Code of Conduct 2011;
- SRA Accounts Rules 2011;
- Money Laundering Regulations 2007;
- Data Protection Act 1998;
- Bribery Act 2010;
- Financial Services Act 2000; and
- health and safety regulations.

Documents supporting the compliance plan

[*It is likely that you will wish to limit access to some or all of the following documents rather than making them accessible to all staff.*]

- Risk register (located at [page [ ]/*insert link*])

    - Reviewed and updated by the COLP annually.

- Gap analysis (located at [page [ ]/*insert link*])

    - Reviewed and updated by the COLP annually.

- Monthly compliance monitoring form (located at [page [ ]/*insert link*])

    - Completed by the COLP once a month.

- Business continuity plan (located at [page [ ]/*insert link*])

    - Reviewed and updated by the COLP annually.

- Record of COLP and complaints partner meetings (located at [page [ ]/*insert link*])

    - Monthly meetings to review complaints.
    - Meetings recorded by the COLP.

- Breach report form (located at [page [ ]/*insert link*])

    - Completed and submitted by any employee to the COLP upon realising a breach of compliance has occurred.

- Breach register (located at [page [ ]/*insert link*])
  - Updated by the COLP every time he/she is notified of a breach.

- Breach review form (located at [page [ ]/*insert link*])
  - Completed by the COLP once a month.
  - Reviewed by the COLP annually and updated as he/she sees fit to ensure its effectiveness.

- Record of reports submitted to the SRA (located at [page [ ]/*insert link*])
  - Updated by the COLP every time he/she submits a breach report to the SRA.

- Whistle-blowing policy (located at [page [ ]/*insert link*])
  - Reviewed and updated by the COLP annually.

Failure to follow compliance plan

The firm is under an obligation to notify the SRA of all breaches of compliance, both material and non-material. The firm takes this obligation seriously and, as such, has implemented policies and procedures to ensure compliance. [Such policies can be found at [page [ ]/*insert link*].] Where compliance is not achieved, we also have a policy to notify the COLP of the breach. Failure to comply with the firm's compliance plan and its policies and procedures is a disciplinary offence and will be dealt with under the firm's disciplinary procedure.

Review

To ensure that the compliance plan remains up to date and effective, this policy will be formally reviewed every year by the COLP.

Signed: *[Signature of COLP]* _____

Position: _____

Date: _____

Annex 3B

Risk register

Note: This risk register is provided on the CD-Rom which accompanies this toolkit as a Microsoft Excel spreadsheet. We recommend that each department completes its own risk register, with the COLP taking overall control. The spreadsheet includes tabs for the following departments: compliance; the board; finance; HR; marketing; IT and the various business lines/practice areas. It can then be adapted to suit the firm's business needs.

Risk identified	Potential con-sequences	Impact (high/ medium/ low)	Probability (high/ medium/ low)	Overall risk (high/ medium/ low)	Response	Action plan	Owner	Delivery date	Review date	Notes

Annex 3C

Compliance gap analysis

Note: This is an example gap analysis only. You and your firm must decide what aspects of your business need to be analysed. We provide the following headings as suggestions only.

	Do you understand the requirements sufficiently?	What further work/help is required to reach an understanding?	Do you currently meet this requirement?	Where are you short on this requirement?	Action required to address any gap	When do you envisage you will be able to meet this requirement?	Who will be responsible for actions on this requirement?	Estimated time required to address gap	Level of resource needed to address gap
SRA Code of Conduct 2011									
Chapter 1: Client care									
Chapter 2: Equality and diversity									
Chapter 3: Conflicts of interests									
Chapter 4: Confidentiality and disclosure									
Chapter 5: Your client and the court									
Chapter 6: Your client and introductions to third parties									
Chapter 7: Management of your business									
Chapter 8: Publicity									
Chapter 9: Fee sharing and referrals									
Chapter 10: You and your regulator									
Chapter 11: Relations with third parties									
Chapter 12: Separate businesses									
Regulatory compliance									
Practising certificate requirements									
Professional Indemnity Insurance (PII)									

	Do you understand the requirements sufficiently?	What further work/help is required to reach an understanding?	Do you currently meet this requirement?	Where are you short on this requirement?	Action required to address any gap	When do you envisage you will be able to meet this requirement?	Who will be responsible for actions on this requirement?	Estimated time required to address gap	Level of resource needed to address gap
SRA Authorisation Rules 2011									
Internal audits									
External audits									
Statutory compliance									
Money Laundering Regulations 2007									
Data Protection Act 1998									
Legal Services Act 2007									
Discrimination, equality and diversity policy									
Health and safety policy									
Bribery Act 2010									
Financial control									
Financial Services Authority (FSA) rules									
SRA Accounts Rules 2011									
Business continuity									
Contingency plan for loss of key personnel									
Contingency plan for catastrophic event									
Governance									
Governance framework									
Training requirements									
CPD requirements									
Trainee requirements									

Annex 3D
Monthly compliance monitoring form

Month of review:	
Name of reviewer:	
Overview of financial reports – cash flow; fees; credit control:	
Complaints:	
Client feedback:	
Risk issues – high risk matters; claims; circumstances:	
File reviews and audits – significant findings:	
Undertakings:	
Equality and diversity; anti-discrimination:	
Health and safety:	
IT security and data protection:	
Referral arrangements:	

Signed: _[signature of COLP]_

Dated:

Annex 3E
Record of meetings with complaints partner

Date of meeting:
Attendees:
Agenda: • Review any new complaints received. • Review existing complaints. Are they being handled promptly, fairly and openly? How can they be resolved? • Identify any trends. • Identify any necessary improvements to systems/procedures. • Identify any training needs.
Actions agreed:
Date of next meeting:

4 Reporting to the SRA

Under the SRA Authorisation Rules the firm and/or the COLP is required to provide an annual information report containing such information as may be specified 'in the prescribed form and by the prescribed date' (rule 8.7(a)). The COLP or the firm must also report the following:

- any change in the information provided in an application for authorisation (rule 3.1(b));
- any material non-compliance with the SRA Handbook (rule 8.5(c)(ii));
- any changes to relevant information about the firm, its employees, managers or interest holders (rule 8.7(c));
- anything which suggests that the firm has, or may have, provided the SRA with information which was or may have been false, misleading, incomplete or inaccurate, or has or may have changed in a material way (rule 8.7(d));
- becoming the sole active partner of a partnership, in the event that they are the sole active partner by reason of the imprisonment, incapacity or the imposition of relevant conditions on, or abandonment of the practice by, the other partner or partners (rule 8.8);
- the loss of the sole remaining solicitor or registered European lawyer (REL) whose role ensured the status of the body as a legal services body (rule 8.9);
- the loss of the sole remaining authorised individual whose role enabled the body to be a licensable body (rule 8.10);
- that the firm ceases to have an approved COLP (rule 18); and
- any unforeseen temporary breach of conditions of a partnership where temporary emergency recognition of a sole practitioner or new firm is required (rules 24 and 25).

The firm is also responsible for making an application for temporary emergency authorisation of a COLP when appropriate (rule 18).

While many of these requirements are placed on the authorised body directly, in most cases it will be the COLP who will take on the role of reporting these issues to the SRA. If the authorised body does not want the COLP to take on some of its reporting responsibilities – for example, it may be more appropriate for HR to report any changes to managers or interest holders – the firm should ensure that the responsibility for such tasks is clearly documented. The Law Society has created a document summarising the SRA reporting requirements: **www.lawsociety.org.uk/ new/documents/practicesupport/reportingrequirements.pdf**.

4.1 Recording

COLPs will be required to report all breaches of compliance, at one point or another, to the SRA. In order to do so the COLP must keep contemporaneous records of all breaches. The best way of doing this will depend on the culture and structure of the firm. One way might be for employees to complete a breach report form and give it to the COLP (see **Annex 4A**). Another way would be for employees to report breaches orally/by email to the COLP who will then fill in the breach register directly (see **Annex 4B**).

Regardless of the method used to inform the COLP of breaches, the COLP will need to have a centralised reporting system to allow them to capture and record all breaches in compliance.

The data should be captured in such a way that patterns of breaches can be identified. We recommend that the COLP reviews the breaches reported on a monthly basis and looks for patterns.

The COLP may also need to consider whether the breach is a 'notifiable circumstance' for insurance purposes. If another person is responsible for claims and complaints, the COLP will need to liaise with that person closely. They will also need to liaise with the COFA.

4.2 The COLP's reporting requirements

The SRA requires reports from the COLP in two circumstances:

1. Material breaches should be reported as soon as reasonably practicable on an ad hoc basis.
2. Rule 8.7 of the SRA Authorisation Rules requires firms to submit an annual information report to the SRA, which must include details of non-material breaches.

> **Note:** When the toolkit went to print a draft annual information report was not available; however, it is understood that initially the annual information report questions will be similar to those required by insurers on PII renewal.

When deciding if a breach is material, the COLP must consider:

- whether there is a detriment, or risk of a detriment, to the client;
- the extent of the risk of loss of confidence in the practice or in the provision of legal services;
- the scale of the issue; and
- the overall impact on the practice, its clients and third parties.

It is important to note that a series of minor breaches can therefore amount to a material breach under this test. It is for this reason that the COLP should have systems in place to identify patterns of breaches.

It will be important for the COLP to ensure that the firm has an open door culture. The COLP will only be able to meet their obligations if fee earners and support staff feel able to report breaches. To aid this, firms should consider having a whistle-blowing policy (see IB(10.10) of the SRA Code of Conduct and **Annex 4F**).

4.3 How to report

The enforcement section of the SRA website contains a 'Report form' which could be used (**www.sra.org.uk/solicitors/enforcement/solicitor-report/other-solicitor-results.page**). Reports can also be made by email, phone or via the SRA's Red Alert line. A further alternative is to speak to the firm's relationship manager at the SRA (if appropriate). A draft reporting letter to the SRA can be found at **Annex 4C**.

Non-material breaches will be reported to the SRA in the annual information report as required under rule 8.7 of the SRA Authorisation Rules. At the time of going to print, it is expected that the SRA will issue further information on its strategy for regulatory reporting and notifications.

4.4 Reviewing breaches

Whilst many may view the task of recording and reporting breaches as a 'necessary evil', it is also very worthwhile as part of effective compliance management for the firm. The key is to consider the data which is being compiled and make it useful to the firm as well as to the SRA. We recommend that, on a monthly basis, the breach record is reviewed. If used effectively, the data can identify areas where fee earners and/or support staff require training, show patterns of minor breaches which must be reported as a material breach, and highlight where improvements are needed to current systems and procedures.

Annex 4A
Internal breach report form

Date of report:		Client reference:	
Date of breach:		Name of employee reporting (or anonymous):	
Name(s) of employee(s) involved:		Name of department(s) involved:	
Type of breach (if known):			
Brief description of breach:			
Suggested action to remedy:			
Has the client been affected by the breach? If so, how?			
Does the client need to be informed of the breach? [NB consider in conjunction with insurers]			
Has there been a complaint as a result of the breach? If so, please give details.			
Employee signature:			
COLP signature:			
Has the breach register been updated?	Yes/No		

Annex 4B

Breach register

Note: By adopting a key such as the one provided below, the breach register also becomes a useful tool for collecting management information (MI). The MI can then be used to identify areas of weakness in the firm. For example, if the majority of breaches relate to Principle 5 of the SRA Handbook (HP5), it is evident that the firm's staff need further training on client care issues.

	Date of breach	Date breach reported to COLP	Type of breach (see key)	Name of employee/department	Has the breach been remedied? If so, how?	Was the breach preventable?	Is the breach reportable to the SRA now? (Is it a material breach?)	If not, why not?	Date breach reported to the SRA	Current position re. report to SRA
1										
2										
3										
4										
5										
6										
7										
8										
9										
10										

Key	
Type of breach	**Reference**
SRA Handbook Principle X	HP Principle reference
SRA Code of Conduct 2011 outcome (X.X)	CCO(outcome reference)
SRA Accounts Rules 2011	AR
Internal policy	IP
Money Laundering Regulations 2007	MLR
Data Protection Act 1998	DPA
Financial Services Act 2000	FSA
Health and safety regulations	H&S
Undertakings	U

Annex 4C
Draft letter to the SRA reporting a material breach

[Firm's contact details]

Solicitors Regulation Authority
Ipsley Court
Berrington Close
Redditch
Worcestershire
B98 0TD

[Date]

Your ref: *[SRA ref]*
Our ref: *[internal ref]*

Dear Sirs

I write to you in my capacity as COLP, on behalf of my firm, *[name of firm]*, as required under rule 8.5(e) of the SRA Authorisation Rules 2011, to inform you of the following material failure[s] to comply with *[state the principle, outcome or statutory reference]*.

I have deemed the failure to be a material breach on account of [the volume of instances of non-compliance with *[principle, outcome or statutory reference]*/its resulting in detriment or risk of detriment to a client/the scale of the issue/the overall impact it has had on the practice, its clients and third parties].

The history of the breach[es] giving rise to this failure is set out below:

[Provide succinct history covering:

- *timing of breach(es) and discovery;*
- *nature of breach(es);*
- *outcome, principle or statutory requirement breached;*
- *whether breach(es) resulted in any loss or detriment to the client;*
- *cause of breach(es);*
- *status of rectification of error/deficiency in procedures/processes giving rise to breach(es), if applicable;*
- *any recompense given to clients; and*
- *any disciplinary action taken as a result of breach(es) or remedial action to reduce the risk of reoccurrence in the future].*

Should you require any further information in respect of the above matter please do not hesitate to contact me.

Yours faithfully

[*Signature of COLP*]

[*Printed name and position of COLP*]

Annex 4D
Breach review form

Date of review:	
Name of reviewer:	
Have there been any breaches reported?	
If so, how many and what are they?	
Is this an increase or decrease from last month?	
Which departments have the breaches occurred in?	
How many breaches in these departments have been reported over the past year?	
Is a specific employee committing a lot of breaches?	
Is any training required?	
Do any new procedures need to be implemented?	
Do any existing policies/ procedures need to be amended?	
Are there any patterns?	
Date of next review:	

Annex 4E
Record of reports submitted to SRA

Note: Examples of results could include: acknowledged and awaiting allocation; under investigation; investigation concluded – no further action; investigation concluded – disciplinary sanction; SDT proceedings.

Breach number / file reference	Date reported	Type of breach	Employee involved	Result
1				
2				
3				
4				
5				
6				

Annex 4F
Whistle-blowing policy

Date created:	
Date reviewed:	

1   Policy statement

1.1 We are committed to conducting our business with honesty and integrity, and expect all staff to maintain high standards in accordance with the SRA Handbook. However, we are aware that we face the risk of things going wrong from time to time, or of unknowingly harbouring illegal or unethical conduct. A culture of openness and accountability is essential in order to prevent such situations occurring or to address them when they do occur.

1.2 The aims of this policy are:

(a)   to encourage staff to report suspected wrongdoing as soon as possible;

(b)   to provide staff with guidance as to how to raise those concerns;

(c)   to reassure staff that they are able to raise genuine concerns in good faith without fear of reprisals, even if they turn out to be mistaken.

1.3 This policy does not form part of any employee's contract of employment and it may be amended at any time.

2   Who is covered by this policy?

2.1 This policy applies to any and all individuals working at any and all levels of the firm (collectively referred to as 'staff' in this policy).

3   What is whistle-blowing?

3.1 'Whistle-blowing' is the disclosure of information which relates to suspected wrongdoing or dangers at work. This may include:

(a)   criminal activity;

(b)   miscarriages of justice;

(c)   danger to health and safety;

(d)   damage to the environment;

(e)   failure to comply with any legal or professional obligations or regulatory requirements, including the SRA Code of Conduct 2011 and SRA Accounts Rules 2011;

(f)   bribery;

(g)   financial fraud or mismanagement;

(h)   negligence;

(i)   breach of our internal policies and procedures;

(j)   conduct likely to damage our reputation;

(k)   unauthorised disclosure of confidential information;

(l)   the deliberate concealment of any of the above matters.

3.2 A 'whistle-blower' is a person who raises a genuine concern in good faith relating to any of the above. If you have any genuine concerns related to suspected wrongdoing or danger affecting any of our activities (a 'whistle-blowing concern') you should report it under this policy.

3.3 If you are uncertain whether something is within the scope of this policy you should seek advice from the compliance officer for legal practice (COLP), whose contact details are at the end of this policy.

4   Raising a whistle-blowing concern

4.1 We hope that in many cases you will be able to raise any concerns with your supervisor. You may tell them in person or put the matter in writing if you prefer. They may be able to agree a way of resolving your concern quickly and effectively. In some cases they may refer the matter to the COLP.

4.2 However, where the matter is more serious, or you feel that your supervisor has not addressed your concern, or you prefer not to raise it with them for any reason, please contact the COLP, whose contact details are at the end of this policy.

5   Confidentiality

5.1 We hope that staff will feel able to voice whistle-blowing concerns openly under this policy. However, if you want to raise your concern confidentially, we will make every effort to keep your identity secret. If it is necessary for anyone investigating your concern to know your identity, we will discuss this with you.

5.2 We do not encourage staff to make disclosures anonymously. Proper investigation may be more difficult or impossible if we cannot obtain further information from you. It is also more difficult to establish whether any allegations are credible and have been made in good faith. Whistle-blowers who are concerned about possible reprisals if their identity is revealed should come forward to the COLP and appropriate measures can then be taken to preserve confidentiality.

6   External disclosures

6.1 The aim of this policy is to provide an internal mechanism for reporting, investigating and remedying any wrongdoing in the workplace. In most cases you should not find it necessary to alert anyone externally.

6.2 The law recognises that in some circumstances it may be appropriate for you to report your concerns to an external body such as a regulator. It will very rarely if ever be appropriate to alert the media. We strongly encourage you to seek advice before reporting a concern to anyone external.

6.3 Whistle-blowing concerns usually relate to the conduct of our staff, but they may sometimes relate to the actions of a third party, such as a client, supplier or service provider. The law allows you to raise a concern in good faith with a third party, where you reasonably believe it relates mainly to their actions or something that is legally their responsibility. However, we encourage you to report such concerns internally first. You should contact your supervisor or the COLP for guidance.

7   Investigation and outcome

7.1 Once you have raised a concern, we will carry out an initial assessment to determine the scope of any investigation. We will inform you of the outcome of our assessment. You may be required to attend additional meetings in order to provide further information.

7.2 We will aim to keep you informed of the progress of the investigation and its likely timescale. However, sometimes the need for confidentiality may prevent us giving you specific details of the investigation or any disciplinary action taken as a result. You should treat any information about the investigation as confidential.

7.3 If we conclude that a whistle-blower has made false allegations maliciously, in bad faith or with a view to personal gain, the whistle-blower will be subject to disciplinary action.

8   If you are not satisfied

8.1 While we cannot always guarantee the outcome you are seeking, we will try to deal with your concern fairly and in an appropriate way. By using this policy you can help us to achieve this.

8.2 If you are not happy with the way in which your concern has been handled, you can raise it with one of the [directors/partners/managers] of the firm.

9   Protection and support for whistle-blowers

9.1 Whistle-blowers are sometimes worried about possible repercussions. We aim to encourage openness and will support staff who raise genuine concerns in good faith under this policy, even if they turn out to be mistaken.

9.2 Staff must not suffer any detrimental treatment as a result of raising a concern in good faith. Detrimental treatment includes dismissal, disciplinary action, threats or other unfavourable treatment connected with raising a concern. If you believe that you have suffered any such treatment, you should inform the COLP immediately. If the matter is not remedied you should raise it formally using our grievance procedure.

9.3 Staff must not threaten or retaliate against whistle-blowers in any way. Anyone involved in such conduct will be subject to disciplinary action.

10 Responsibility for the success of this policy

10.1   The [board of directors/partners of the firm/managers of the firm] [has/have] overall responsibility for this policy, and for reviewing the effectiveness of actions taken in response to concerns raised under this policy.

10.2   The COLP has day-to-day operational responsibility for this policy, and must ensure that all managers and other staff who may deal with concerns or investigations under this policy receive regular and appropriate training.

10.3   The COLP, in conjunction with the board, should review this policy from a legal and operational perspective at least once a year.

10.4   All staff are responsible for the success of this policy and should ensure that they use it to disclose any suspected danger or wrongdoing. Staff are invited to comment on this policy and suggest ways in which it might be improved. Comments, suggestions and queries should be addressed to the COLP.

11 Contacts

COLP

[Name]

[Telephone number]

[Email address]

COFA

[Name]

[Telephone number]

[Email address]

[Managing/senior partner]

[Name]

[Telephone number]

[Email address]

[External auditors]

[Name]

[Telephone number]

[Email address]

APPENDIX A

SRA Authorisation Rules 2011 (extracts)

Part 3: Conditions of authorisation

...

Rule 8: General conditions on authorisation

...

8.5 Compliance officers

(a) An authorised body must have suitable arrangements in place to ensure that its compliance officers are able to discharge their duties in accordance with these rules.

(b) An authorised body must at all times have an individual:

 (i) who is a manager or an employee of the authorised body;
 (ii) who is designated as its COLP;
 (iii) who is of sufficient seniority and in a position of sufficient responsibility to fulfil the role; and
 (iv) whose designation is approved by the SRA.

(c) The COLP of an authorised body must:

 (i) take all reasonable steps to:

 (A) ensure compliance with the terms and conditions of the authorised body's authorisation except any obligations imposed under the SRA Accounts Rules;
 (B) ensure compliance with any statutory obligations of the body, its managers, employees or interest holders in relation to the body's carrying on of authorised activities; and
 (C) record any failure so to comply and make such records available to the SRA on request; and

 (ii) as soon as reasonably practicable, report to the SRA any failure so to comply, provided that:

 (A) in the case of non-material failures, these shall be taken to have been reported as soon as reasonably practicable if they are reported to the SRA together with such other information as the SRA may require in accordance with Rule 8.7(a); and
 (B) a failure may be material either taken on its own or as part of a pattern of failures so to comply.

(d) An authorised body must at all times have an individual:

    (i) who is a manager or an employee of the authorised body;

    (ii) who is designated as its COFA;

    (iii) who is of sufficient seniority and in a position of sufficient responsibility to fulfil the role; and

    (iv) whose designation is approved by the SRA.

(e) The COFA of an authorised body must:

    (i) take all reasonable steps to:

        (A) ensure that the body and its employees and managers comply with any obligations imposed upon them under the SRA Accounts Rules;

        (B) record any failure so to comply and make such records available to the SRA on request; and

    (ii) as soon as reasonably practicable, report to the SRA any failure so to comply, provided that:

        (A) in the case of non-material failures, these shall be taken to have been reported as soon as reasonably practicable if they are reported to the SRA together with such other information as the SRA may require in accordance with Rule 8.7(a); and

        (B) a failure may be material either taken on its own or as part of a pattern of failures so to comply.

(f) The SRA may approve an individual's designation as a COLP or COFA if it is satisfied, in accordance with Part 4, that the individual is a suitable person to carry out his or her duties.

(g) A designation of an individual as a COLP or COFA has effect only while the individual:

    (i) consents to the designation;

    (ii) in the case of a COLP:

        (A) is not disqualified from acting as a HOLP; and

        (B) is:

            (I) a lawyer of England and Wales;

            (II) an REL; or

            (III) registered with the BSB under Regulation 17 of the European Communities (Lawyer's Practice) Regulations 2000 (SI 2000/1119);

        and is an authorised person in relation to one or more of the reserved legal activities which the body is authorised to carry on; and

    (iii) in the case of a COFA, is not disqualified from acting as a HOFA.

...

Part 4: Approval of managers, owners and compliance officers

Rule 13: Application for approval

13.1 This Part governs the SRA's determination of applications for:

(a) approval of an authorised body's managers and owners pursuant to Rule 8.6(a); and

(b) approval of an authorised body's compliance officers, pursuant to Rule 8.5(b) and (d).

13.2 The SRA will deem a person to be approved as suitable to be a manager or owner of an authorised body under this Part if:

(a) that person is:

(i) a solicitor who holds a current practising certificate; or

(ii) an authorised body;

(b) there is no condition on the person's practising certificate or authorisation as appropriate, preventing or restricting them from being a manager, owner or interest holder of an authorised body or being a sole practitioner;

(c) the SRA is notified on the prescribed form in advance of the person becoming a manager or owner of the authorised body; and

(d) the SRA has not withdrawn its approval of that person to be a manager or owner under Rule 17.

Rule 14: Approval process

14.1 An application for approval of a manager, owner or compliance officer may be made by an applicant body or an authorised body and must include evidence to satisfy the SRA that the candidate is suitable to be a manager, owner or compliance officer of the body, as appropriate.

14.2 The applicant body or authorised body, as appropriate, must:

(a) co-operate, and secure the co-operation of the candidate, to assist the SRA to obtain all information and documentation the SRA requires in order to determine the application;

(b) obtain all other information and documentation in relation to the candidate which the prescribed form requires the body to obtain and keep; and

(c) keep all information and documentation under (b) above for a period of not less than 6 years after the person concerned has ceased to be a manager, owner or compliance officer of the body.

14.3 The candidate must declare in the application that the information supplied about them is correct and complete.

14.4 The SRA's decision to approve or refuse approval must be notified in writing to the applicant body or authorised body as appropriate, and separately to the candidate, as soon as possible.

14.5 The SRA may, at the time of granting its approval or at any time subsequently:

   (a)   approve the holding of a material interest in a licensed body subject to conditions in accordance with paragraphs 17, 28 or 33 of Schedule 13 to the LSA [Legal Services Act 2007]; and

   (b)   make its approval of a person to be an owner, manager or compliance officer of an authorised body subject to such conditions on the body's authorisation as it considers appropriate having regard to the criteria in Rule 9.

14.6 If the SRA proposes to object to a candidate becoming an owner of an applicant body or authorised body, or to approve such a person becoming an owner subject to conditions imposed under Rule 14.5(a) or (b), the SRA must:

   (a)   give the candidate and the body a warning notice which:

      (i)   specifies the SRA's intention to object or to impose conditions; and

      (ii) states that any representations must be made to the SRA within the period of 28 days from the date of the notice; and

   (b)   consider any representations made to the SRA by the body and/or the candidate within the 28 day period in (a)(ii) above.

14.7 The SRA may issue a conditional approval or objection without a warning notice under Rule 14.6 if the application for approval has been made after the grant of authorisation and the SRA considers it necessary or desirable to dispense with the warning notice for the purpose of protecting any of the regulatory objectives.

14.8 The SRA may at any time require the production of information or documentation from:

   (a)   a person who has been approved as an owner, manager or compliance officer under this Part;

   (b)   an authorised body of which that person is a manager, owner or compliance officer; or

   (c)   the body which originally obtained approval for that person and holds information and documentation under Rule 14.2(c);

in order to satisfy the SRA that the person met, meets, or continues to meet the criteria for approval.

Guidance notes

   (i)   See also the guidance notes to Rule 1 regarding ownership and material interest.

   (ii) The SRA's notification "in writing" includes any form of written electronic communication normally used for business purposes, such as emails.

  (iii) See also Regulation 7 of the SRA Practising Regulations under which the SRA has the power to impose conditions on a practising certificate or registration which restrict an individual's ability to be involved in an authorised body.

  (iv) Specific provisions exist in the LSA about imposing conditions on the approval of owners of a licensed body:

(a) For the approval of ownership on an application for a licence, see paragraph 17 of Schedule 13 to the LSA. For the approval of ownership on a change of interests after a licence is issued, see paragraph 28 of that Schedule. These give the SRA the power to approve an owner's or a prospective owner's holding subject to conditions where the Rule 15 criteria are not met in relation to that investment, but only if the SRA considers that, if the conditions are complied with, it will be appropriate for the owner to hold the interest.

(b) For the imposition of conditions (or further conditions) on an existing ownership interest, see paragraph 33 of Schedule 13 to the LSA. This gives the SRA the power to impose conditions (or further conditions) on a person's holding of an interest, if the SRA is not satisfied that the Rule 15 criteria are met, or if the SRA is satisfied that a condition imposed under paragraphs 17, 28 or 33 of Schedule 13 (see above) on the person's holding of that interest has not been, or is not being, complied with. The SRA may only use the paragraph 33 power if it considers that, if the conditions are complied with, it will be appropriate for the owner to hold the interest without the approval requirements being met.

Rule 15: Criteria for approval

15.1 When considering whether a candidate should be approved to be a manager, owner or compliance officer of the body, as appropriate, the SRA will take into account the criteria set out in the SRA Suitability Test and any other relevant information.

Guidance notes

(i) As well as evidence about the candidate, the Suitability Test takes into account evidence about the honesty and integrity of a person that the candidate is related to, affiliated with, or acts together with where the SRA has reason to believe that that person may have an influence over the way in which the candidate will exercise their role.

(ii) Under paragraphs 19 and 20 of Schedule 13 to the LSA the SRA has the power, when dealing with an application for a licence, to object to the holding of an interest if it is not satisfied that the Rule 15 criteria are met in relation to that holding. The mechanism for objecting is set out in those paragraphs.

Rule 16: Effect of approval

16.1 Approval takes effect from the date of the decision unless otherwise stated and remains effective only if the candidate takes up the position for which he or she has been approved within the period specified in the notice of approval.

16.2 Subject to Rule 16.1, approval continues until:

(a) it is withdrawn by the SRA; or

(b) the approved person ceases to be a manager, interest holder, COLP or COFA of the authorised body, as appropriate.

Guidance note

(i) The period specified in the notice of approval in Rule 16.1 will normally be 90 days although may be varied in individual cases.

Rule 17: Withdrawal of approval

17.1 Where the SRA has granted an approval of a person to be a manager, owner or compliance officer of a body (including a deemed approval under Rule 13.2), it may subsequently withdraw that approval if:

(a) it is not satisfied that an approved person met or meets the criteria for approval in Rule 15;

(b) it is satisfied that a condition imposed on the body's authorisation under Rule 14.5 has not been, or is not being complied with;

(c) it is satisfied that the approved person has breached a duty or obligation imposed upon them in or under the SRA's regulatory arrangements or any enactments; or

(d) information or documentation is not promptly supplied in response to a request made under Rule 14.8.

17.2 Where withdrawal of approval relates to a director of a company, the SRA may set separate dates for that individual ceasing to be a director and disposing of his or her shares.

Rule 18: Temporary emergency approvals for compliance officers

18.1 If an authorised body ceases to have a COLP or COFA whose designation has been approved by the SRA, the authorised body must immediately and in any event within seven days:

(a) notify the SRA;

(b) designate another manager or employee to replace its previous COLP or COFA, as appropriate; and

(c) make an application to the SRA for temporary approval of the new COLP or COFA, as appropriate.

18.2 The SRA may grant a temporary approval under this rule if:

(a) it is satisfied that the authorised body could not reasonably have commenced an application for approval of designation in advance of the non-compliance; and

(b) on the face of the application and any other information immediately before the SRA, there is no evidence suggesting that the new compliance officer is not suitable to carry out the duties imposed on them under these rules.

18.3 Temporary approval under this rule:

(a) may be granted initially for 28 days;

(b) may be granted to have effect from the date the body ceases to have a COLP or COFA whose designation has been approved;

(c) may be extended in response to a reasonable request by the authorised body;

(d) must be extended pending determination of a substantive application for approval commenced in accordance with Rule 18.4;

(e) may be granted or extended subject to such conditions on the authorised body's authorisation as the SRA thinks fit, having regard to the criteria in Rule 9;

(f) has effect only while the criteria in Rule 8.5(g) are met;

(g) if granted, cannot prejudice the discretion of the SRA to refuse a substantive application for approval of designation or to impose any conditions on that approval; and

(h) in exceptional circumstances, and for reasonable cause, may be withdrawn at any time.

18.4 If granted temporary approval under Rule 18.3 above for its designation of a new COLP or COFA, the authorised body must:

(a) designate a permanent COLP or COFA, as appropriate; and

(b) submit a substantive application for approval of that designation under Rule 13;

before the expiry of the temporary approval or any extension of that approval by the SRA.

APPENDIX B

SRA Suitability Test 2011

Introduction to the Suitability Test

Preamble

Authority: Made on 17 June 2011 by the Solicitors Regulation Authority Board under sections 28, 79 and 80 of the Solicitors Act 1974 with the approval of the Legal Services Board under paragraph 19 of Schedule 4 to the Legal Services Act 2007

Date: These regulations came into force on 6 October 2011

Replacing: The SRA guidelines on the assessment of character and suitability

Applicability: Students and trainee solicitors under the SRA Training Regulations;

Qualified lawyers under the QLTSR;

Those seeking admission as solicitors under the Admission Regulations, fulfilling the duties under section 3 of the Solicitors Act 1974;

Those seeking to become authorised role holders in accordance with rules 8.5 and 8.6 of the SRA Authorisation Rules and regulation 4.8 of the SRA Practising Regulations;

Those seeking restoration to the roll of solicitors under regulation 8 of the Solicitors Keeping of the Roll Regulations 2011.

Overview

Outcomes-focused regulation concentrates on providing positive outcomes which when achieved will benefit and protect *clients* and the public. We must ensure that any individual admitted as a *solicitor* has, and maintains, the level of honesty, integrity and the professionalism expected by the public and other stakeholders and professionals, and does not pose a risk to the public or the profession.

The Suitability Test will apply the same high standards to all those seeking admission or restoration to the roll as a *solicitor*, as well as legally qualified and non-legally qualified applicants for roles in authorised bodies as *authorised role holders*.

The test is the same for non-solicitors as they will be working within the profession and must meet the same high standards that the general public expect of *solicitors*. This document is intended to make it clear to *you* what this standard is in terms of *your* character, suitability, fitness and propriety.

No applicant has the automatic right of admission, restoration or authorisation and it will always be for *you* to discharge the burden of satisfying suitability under this test. Any application that requires *us* to be satisfied as to character, suitability, fitness and propriety will be determined by reference to this test.

The Principles

The Suitability Test forms part of the Handbook, in which the 10 mandatory *Principles* are all-pervasive. They apply to all those *we* regulate and to all aspects of practice.

You must:

1 uphold the rule of law and the proper administration of justice;
2 act with integrity;
3 not allow *your* independence to be compromised;
4 act in the best interests of each *client*;
5 provide a proper standard of service to *your clients*;
6 behave in a way that maintains the trust the public places in *you* and in the provision of legal services;
7 comply with *your* legal and regulatory obligations and deal with *your* regulators and ombudsmen in an open, timely and co-operative manner;
8 run *your* business or carry out *your* role in the business effectively and in accordance with proper governance and sound financial and risk management principles;
9 run *your* business or carry out *your* role in the business in a way that encourages equality of opportunity and respect for diversity; and
10 protect *client money* and *assets*.

Outcomes

The outcomes which apply to this test are as follows:

O(SB1) if *you* are a *solicitor*, *you* are of the required standard of *character and suitability*;
O(SB2) if *you* are an *authorised role holder*, *you* are fit and proper; and
O(SB3) *you* act so that *clients*, and the wider public, have confidence that O(SB1) has been demonstrated.

The outcomes, and the criteria that flow from them, apply to all those who are intending to become *solicitors* – i.e. students, *trainee solicitors*, and qualified lawyers from other jurisdictions seeking qualification via transfer – at the point of *student enrolment*, admission, and throughout the pre-qualification period. They also apply to *compliance officers*, *owners*, and/or *managers* at the point of and throughout their period of authorisation, and for former *solicitors* seeking restoration to the roll.

Interpretation and definitions

1   The SRA Handbook Glossary 2012 shall apply and, unless the context otherwise requires:

(a)   all italicised terms shall be defined; and

(b)   all terms shall be interpreted;

in accordance with the *Glossary*.

2   In this test, the reference in the preamble to those seeking to become *authorised role holders* in accordance with rules 8.5 and 8.6 of the *SRA Authorisation Rules*, fulfilling the duties under Sections 89, 90, 91 and 92 of the *LSA* shall have no effect until such time as the Society is designated as a licensing authority under Part 1 of Schedule 10 to the *LSA*.

3   This test shall not apply to licensed bodies until such time as the Society is designated as a licensing authority under Part 1 of Schedule 10 to the *LSA* and all definitions shall be construed accordingly.

4   Part 2 of this test shall have no effect until such time as the Society is designated as a licensing authority under Part 1 of Schedule 10 to the *LSA*.

Part 1: Basic requirements

If *you* are applying for *student enrolment*, admission or restoration to the roll, *you* must comply with Part 1. If *you* are applying for authorisation as an *authorised role holder* then *you* must comply with Part 1 and Part 2.

When considering any application under this test, *we* will take the following actions:

1: Criminal offences

1.1   Unless there are exceptional circumstances, *we* will refuse *your* application if *you* have been convicted by a *court* of a criminal offence:

(a)   for which *you* received a custodial or suspended sentence;

(b)   involving dishonesty, fraud, perjury and/or bribery;

(c)   specifically in relation to which *you* have been included on the Violent and Sex Offender Register;

(d)   associated with obstructing the course of justice;

(e)   which demonstrated behaviour showing signs of *discrimination* towards others;

(f)   associated with terrorism;

(g)   which was racially aggravated;

(h)   which was motivated by any of the 'protected' characteristics defined within the Equality Act 2010;

(i) which in *our* judgement is so serious as to prevent *your student enrolment*, admission as a *solicitor*, or approval as an *authorised role holder*; and/or

(j) *you* have been convicted by a *court* of more than one criminal offence.

Guidance note

(i) The provisions in 1.1(a) will not be relevant to entities because *bodies corporate*, and other unincorporated bodies and bodies of persons, cannot themselves receive custodial sentences.

1.2 *We* are more likely than not to refuse *your* application if *you* have:

(a) been convicted by a *court* of a criminal offence not falling within 1.1 above but which has an impact on *your character and suitability*;

(b) been included on the Violent and Sex Offender Register but in relation to *your* inclusion on the Register, *you* have not been convicted by a *court* of a criminal offence; and/or

(c) accepted a caution for an offence involving dishonesty.

1.3 *We* may refuse *your* application if *you* have:

(a) received a local warning from the police;

(b) accepted a caution from the police for an offence not involving dishonesty;

(c) received a Penalty Notice for Disorder (PND) from the police;

(d) received a final warning or reprimand from the police (youths only); and/or

(e) received a referral order from the *courts* (youths only).

Guidance note

(i) Where a criminal conviction, warning, simple caution, PND and/or inclusion on the Violent and Sex Offender Register has been disclosed, *we* will not look behind the decision made by the police or the finding made by a *court*. However, *we* will take into account material such as sentencing remarks and any other independent information. See also Section 7 Evidence.

(ii) *You* should disclose details of any criminal charge(s) *you* may be facing. *We* will not determine *your* application until *you* can confirm that the charge(s) has/have either been dropped or the outcome of *your* case is known.

(iii) Cautions and local warnings issued by the police may be subsequently recorded on the Police National Computer (PNC) and these will be shown on a PNC printout, which *you* may be required to submit to *us*.

(iv) Police can only issue a caution if there is evidence that *you* are guilty of an offence and if *you* admit that *you* committed the offence. Therefore, by accepting a caution, please bear in mind that *you* are making an admission of guilt.

(v) On Penalty Notices for Disorder no admission of guilt is required, and by paying the penalty, a recipient discharges liability for conviction for the offence – however, *you* should still disclose such matters as *we* will need to consider them.

(vi) Serious motoring offences that result in a criminal conviction must be disclosed. Motoring offences that do not result in a criminal conviction do not need to be disclosed.

2: Disclosure

2.1 All material information relating to *your* application must be disclosed. Failure to disclose material information will be treated as prima facie evidence of dishonest behaviour.

2.2 *You* must disclose any matters that have occurred in the *UK* and/or overseas.

Guidance note

(i) *You* should bear in mind that Regulation 35 of the *SRA Training Regulations* Part 1 – Qualification Regulations requires all those seeking admission as *solicitors* to apply for a standard disclosure from the Criminal Records Bureau (CRB). *We* will also perform a PNC check at the *student enrolment* stage and have reciprocal arrangements with other jurisdictions in order to gather similar information on lawyers from other countries.

(ii) If *you* are seeking approval as an *authorised role holder*, *you* should bear in mind that Rule 14 of the *SRA Authorisation Rules* allows *us* to seek other information relating to *your* application and this would normally include CRB disclosure.

(iii) It is therefore highly likely that matters will come to light.

3: Behaviour not compatible with that expected of a prospective solicitor or authorised role holder

3.1 Unless there are exceptional circumstances *we* will refuse *your* application if *you* have:

(a) been responsible for behaviour:

(i) which is dishonest;
(ii) which is violent;
(iii) where there is evidence of *discrimination* towards others;

(b) misused *your* position to obtain pecuniary advantage;
(c) misused *your* position of trust in relation to vulnerable people; and/or
(d) been responsible for other forms of behaviour which demonstrate that *you* cannot be relied upon to discharge *your* regulatory duties as a *solicitor* or *authorised role holder*.

4: Assessment offences

4.1 Unless there are exceptional circumstances *we* will refuse *your* application if *you* have committed and/or have been adjudged by an education establishment to have committed a deliberate assessment offence which amounts to plagiarism or cheating to gain an advantage for *yourself* or others.

Guidance note

(i)   Exceptional circumstances may include where the finding does not amount to cheating or dishonesty, e.g. incorrect referencing, or failure to attribute correctly, in an essay or paper.

5: Financial evidence

5.1   Unless there are exceptional circumstances *we* will refuse *your* application if:

(a)   there is evidence that *you* cannot manage *your* finances properly and carefully;

(b)   there is evidence that *you* have deliberately sought to avoid responsibility for *your* debts; and/or

(c)   there is evidence of dishonesty in relation to the management of *your* finances.

5.2   If *you* have been declared bankrupt, entered into any individual voluntary arrangements (IVA) or have had a County Court Judgement issued against *you* it will raise a presumption that there has been evidence that *you* cannot manage *your* finances properly and carefully.

Guidance note

(i)   The following might help to establish confidence in *your* ability to run *your* business/carry out *your* role in the business effectively and in accordance with proper governance and sound financial and risk management principles:

(a)   the bankruptcy/IVA/County Court Judgement occurred many years ago and there is evidence of subsequent sound financial management and conduct to show that creditors have been repaid;

(b)   *you* were affected by exceptional circumstances beyond *your* control which *you* could not have reasonably foreseen.

6: Regulatory history

6.1   Unless there are exceptional circumstances *we* will refuse *your* application if *you*:

(a)   have been made the subject of a serious disciplinary finding, sanction or action by a regulatory body and/or any *court* or other body hearing appeals in relation to disciplinary or regulatory findings;

(b)   have failed to disclose information to a regulatory body when required to do so, or have provided false or misleading information;

(c)   have significantly breached the requirements of a regulatory body;

(d)   have been refused registration by a regulatory body; and/or

(e)   have failed to comply with the reasonable requests of a regulatory body.

6.2   *We* may refuse *your* application if *you* have been rebuked, reprimanded or received a warning about *your* conduct by a regulatory body, unless there are exceptional circumstances.

Guidance note

(i) "Regulatory body" includes *us* and the Solicitors Disciplinary Tribunal, approved regulators under the Legal Services Act 2007, as well as any other body responsible for regulation of a profession.

(ii) *You* should disclose details of any disciplinary proceeding(s) or investigation(s) *you* may be facing. *We* will not determine *your* application until *you* can confirm that the matter(s) has/have either been dropped or the outcome of *your* case is known.

7: *Evidence*

7.1 To help *us* consider an application where a disclosure has been made, *you* should include the following evidence, where relevant:

(a) at least one independent report relating to the event(s), such as sentencing remarks following a criminal conviction;

(b) references from at least two independent professional people (of which one should preferably be from an employer or tutor) who know *you* well and are familiar with the matters being considered;

(c) evidence of any rehabilitation (e.g. probation reports, references from employers and/or tutors);

(d) documentary evidence in support of *your* case and where possible, an independent corroboration of *your* account of the event(s);

(e) *your* attitude towards the event(s);

(f) the extent to which *you* were aware of the rules and procedures governing the reference of material, or the use of group work or collaborative material;

(g) the extent to which *you* could reasonably have been expected to realise that the offence did not constitute legitimate academic practice;

(h) credit check information (in the relevant circumstances); and/or

(i) actions *you* have taken to clear any debts, satisfy any judgements and manage *your* finances.

7.2 The onus is on *you* to provide any evidence *you* consider necessary and/or appropriate. However, should *we* consider that *you* have provided insufficient evidence, *we* reserve the right to carry out *our* own investigation and/or refuse the application if further evidence is not forthcoming.

8: *Rehabilitation*

8.1 It is for *you* to demonstrate that *you* have undergone successful rehabilitation, where relevant. The individual circumstances *you* put forward must be weighed against the public interest and the need to safeguard members of the public and maintain the reputation of the profession. However, *we* will consider each application on its own merits.

8.2 If the Rehabilitation of Offenders Act 1974 (Exceptions) Order 1975 (as amended) is applicable to *your* occupation, profession or role, *you* must declare all convictions and cautions, even if they are deemed to be spent in accordance with the Act.

8.3 In accordance with paragraph 2 above (disclosure), if *you* fall within the Rehabilitation of Offenders Act 1974 (Exceptions) Order 1975 and *you* fail to disclose information about convictions and/or cautions for criminal offences, whether they are spent or unspent, *we* will consider this as amounting to prima facie evidence of dishonest behaviour.

Guidance note

(i) The provisions of the Rehabilitation of Offenders Act 1974 (as amended) and the Rehabilitation of Offenders Act 1974 (Exceptions) Order 1975 (as amended) will be taken into account by *us* in considering any application *you* make.

(ii) If *you* fall within the Rehabilitation of Offenders Act 1974 (Exceptions) Order 1975 (as amended), the fact that the conviction is spent, and the time that has passed since the conviction was given, together with any other material circumstances will be taken into account by *us* when determining any application made by *you*.

(iii) A period of rehabilitation, particularly after *we* have decided to refuse *your* application, will not in itself result in automatic admission/authorisation. *We* need *you* to show, through a period of good behaviour, that *you* have taken steps to rehabilitate *yourself* by *your* own volition.

Part 2: Additional requirements to become authorised under the SRA Authorisation Rules

9: *All applicants must comply with Part 1*

9.1 Under this test, when considering any application by an individual seeking to become an *authorised role holder*, all of the tests set out in Part 1 will apply in addition to this Part.

10: *Additional requirements*

10.1 Unless there are exceptional circumstances *we* may refuse *your* application if:

(a) *you* have been removed from the office of trustee for a charity by an order imposed by the Charities Act 1993;

(b) *you* have been removed and/or disqualified as a company director;

(c) any body corporate of which *you* are/were a *manager* or *owner* has been the subject of a winding up order, an administrative order or an administrative receivership, or has otherwise been wound up or put into administration in circumstances of insolvency;

(d) *you* have a previous conviction which is now spent for a criminal offence relating to bankruptcy, IVAs or other circumstances of insolvency;

(e) *you* are a corporate person/entity subject to a relevant insolvency event defined in rule 1.2 of the *SRA Authorisation Rules*;

(f) *you* are a corporate person/entity and other matters that call *your* fitness and propriety into question are disclosed or come to light;

(g) *you* have committed an offence under the Companies Act 2006; and/or

(h) *we* have evidence reflecting on the honesty and integrity of a person *you* are related to, affiliated with, or act together with where *we* have reason to believe that the person may have an influence over the way in which *you* will exercise *your authorised role*.

Guidance note

(i) The provisions of the Rehabilitation of Offenders Act 1974 (as amended) and the Rehabilitation of Offenders Act 1974 (Exceptions) Order 1975 (as amended) do not apply to corporate persons/entities. Therefore, corporate convictions cannot become spent, so if *you* are a corporate person/entity *you* must disclose any and all matters in *your* application.

(ii) Other matters under 10.1(f) include but are not limited to debts, corporate criminal matters, Companies Act transgressions such as late submission of accounts, and taking steps without submitting proper documents to Companies House.

APPENDIX C

Further guidance

Further guidance available online at the time of printing of this toolkit:

SRA website

- SRA Handbook

  www.sra.org.uk/solicitors/handbook/welcome.page

- Outcomes-focused regulation at a glance

  www.sra.org.uk/solicitors/freedom-in-practice/ofr/ofr-quick-guide.page

- Q&As: Compliance officers for legal practice (COLPs) and compliance officers for finance and administration (COFAs)

  www.sra.org.uk/solicitors/freedom-in-practice/ofr/colp-cofa-questions-answers.page

Law Society website

- Summary of the SRA Handbook reporting requirements

  www.lawsociety.org.uk/new/documents/practicesupport/reportingrequirements.pdf

- Compliance officer FAQs

  www.lawsociety.org.uk/practicesupport/regulation/complianceofficersfaqs.page

- Law Society's practice notes

  - Outcomes-focused regulation: overview

    www.lawsociety.org.uk/productsandservices/practicenotes/ofroverview.page

  - Compliance officers

    www.lawsociety.org.uk/productsandservices/practicenotes/complianceofficers.page

  - Overseas practice

    www.lawsociety.org.uk/productsandservices/practicenotes/overseaspractice.page